THE
WORLD SERIES

MATT CHRISTOPHER®

The #1 Sports Series for Kids

☆ LEGENDARY SPORTS EVENTS ☆

THE
WORLD SERIES

Great Championship Moments

LITTLE, BROWN AND COMPANY
New York ↝ Boston

Little, Brown and Company

Hachette Book Group USA
1271 Avenue of the Americas, New York, NY 10020
Visit our Web site at www.lb-kids.com

www.mattchristopher.com

First Edition: April 2007

Matt Christopher® is a registered trademark of
Matt Christopher Royalties, Inc.

Text written by Stephanie Peters

ISBN-13: 978-0-316-01117-4
ISBN-10: 0-316-01117-7

10 9 8 7 6 5 4 3 2 1

COM-MO

Printed in the United States of America

Contents

Introduction   1

Chapter One: Early 1900s   5
1903–1912: The First World Series,
   Missed Catches, and an Amazing Finish

Chapter Two: 1920s   20
1924: The Big Train Steams to Victory

Chapter Three: 1930s   29
1932: The Legendary Called Shot

Chapter Four: 1940s   37
1947: Seventh-Game Showdown

Chapter Five: 1950s   46
1955: The Dynasty Is Toppled — Once

Chapter Six: 1960s   53
1960: The Pirates Steal the Series

Chapter Seven: 1970s   62
1975: The Best Sixth Game Ever

Chapter Eight: 1980s   71
1988: "Unbelievable!"

Chapter Nine: 1990s   77
1991: The Worst-to-First Classic

Chapter Ten: 2000s   89
2004 and 2005: What Curses?

World Series Results   96

Introduction:
The Road to the First
World Series

Ask baseball fans when their favorite sport was born, and you're likely to get several different answers.

"Alexander J. Cartwright wrote down the first official rules for baseball in 1845," one may say, "and on June 19, 1846, his team, the New York Knickerbockers, played a game by those rules. Since we still follow most of those rules today, that was the first real baseball game."

"But in 1839 in Cooperstown, New York, Abner Doubleday drew a huge diamond in the dirt and put a base down in each corner," another might counter. "That's why it's called *baseball* and why the Baseball Hall of Fame is in Cooperstown."

"The word *baseball* was used long before 1839," a third might object. "A document written in 1791 warns people not to play baseball within 80 yards of the new Pittsfield, Massachusetts, Meeting House. The town was afraid someone would hit a ball through the house's windows!"

"But the game itself was around even earlier than that," a fourth will add. "When George Washington was at Valley Forge during the Revolutionary War, he played an English version of baseball called rounders."

The truth is that modern baseball has no single birthday. It evolved from similar games that used bats and balls and involved running, pitching, throwing, and catching.

What is known, however, is when and how *professional* baseball began. The first baseball team made up entirely of paid athletes, the Cincinnati Red Stockings, was formed in 1869. That team won 56 straight games before being defeated by the amateur Brooklyn Athletics on June 14, 1870.

The Red Stockings' amazing success convinced others to create teams of paid players. On March 17, 1871, nine of these teams were organized into the National Association of Professional Baseball Players (NA). This league lasted only four years before gambling, scandal, and infighting caused it to fold. But on February 2, 1876, a new professional association, the National League (NL), was created.

The NL was a much stronger organization than the NA had been — so strong, in fact, that in 1882, owners of teams that were *not* in the league decided to form a rival organization, the American Association (AA).

The competition between the two leagues was instantaneous and fierce, and at the end of the 1882 season, it came to a head. That September, the NL's number-one squad, the Chicago White Stockings, agreed to play a series of exhibition games against the AA's top team, the Cincinnati Reds. Considered by many to be the first true World Series, the event ended in a tie at one game apiece.

Although there was no rematch in 1883, the two leagues met again in 1884 and continued to meet in the postseason until the AA shuttered its doors at the end of the 1891 season due to financial difficulties.

The NL was not going to be without a rival for long, however. In 1892, sportswriter Byron Bancroft "Ban" Johnson and Reds manager Charlie Comiskey set out to turn a minor baseball organization, the

Western League, into a major-league powerhouse. It took ten years, but by early December 1902, the new organization, the American League, had grown just as strong and as popular as the National League. NL team owners had no choice but to recognize the AL as a major league.

The AL began its first official season in April 1903. By August, one team, the Boston Red Sox (or Pilgrims or Americans, as they were sometimes called), had emerged as the league's standout team. Meanwhile the Pittsburgh Pirates of the NL came out on top for the third season in a row. That same month the Pirates' owner, Barney Dreyfuss, challenged owner Henry Killilea and his Boston squad to a best-of-nine series to determine which team was stronger.

And with that challenge, the World Series was born.

★ CHAPTER ONE ★

EARLY 1900s

1903–1912: The First World Series, Missed Catches, and an Amazing Finish

The 1903 World Series opened on Thursday, October 1, at the Huntington Avenue Baseball Grounds in Boston. Admission cost fifty cents for bleachers or standing room, a dollar for grandstand seats. Spectators near the outfield stood behind ropes.

Warming up were some of baseball's greats, including Pittsburgh's shortstop Honus Wagner and Boston's star pitcher Denton True "Cy" Young. At three o'clock sharp, Young took to the mound. The thirty-six-year-old righty — whose nickname "Cy" was short for "cyclone," after the damage his fastball had once done to some wooden stands — had been playing professional baseball for thirteen years. That season, he had a record of 28 wins, including 7 shutouts and 9 losses, for an earned run average

5

(ERA) of 2.08. His batting average of .321 was just as impressive.

Leading off for the Pirates was Ginger Beaumont. Beaumont was the National League's batting champ that year, with more than 200 hits for the season. This at bat, however, the redheaded slugger sent a fly ball to center field for out number one.

Then Fred Clarke popped up a foul ball. Catcher Lou Criger got under it for the second out. Boston needed just one more to retire the side.

But that last out was a long time coming. First Tommy Leach clocked a ground-rule triple into the roped-off area of the outfield. Then Wagner smashed a single to left. Leach crossed home plate, and the Pirates were on the board.

Things went steadily downhill for Boston after that.

With Kitty Bransfield at the plate, Wagner stole second. Then Bransfield connected on a pitch. The ball bounced along the ground toward second baseman Hobe Ferris. It looked like a sure out — until Ferris fumbled the ball!

Bransfield was safe at first and Wagner advanced to third on the error. Then, as Young threw in the next pitch to batter Claude Ritchey, Bransfield took off for second.

The catcher nabbed the ball, jumped up, and hurled it toward second. The throw was wild! Bransfield bolted for third, and Wagner charged home for the Pirates' second run.

Young walked Ritchey to put runners at first and third. Jimmy Sebring came to bat; and as Young threw in the pitch, Ritchey stole second. Moments later, Sebring pounded out a solid single. Bransfield and Ritchey raced home, and the score jumped to 4–0 with one out yet to go!

That out seemed in the bag when the next batter, Ed Phelps, missed the pitch for his third strike. But Criger, usually so reliable, flubbed the catch! Phelps made it safely to first on the drop-third-strike rule. Luckily for the Red Sox, Young struck out Deacon Phillippe to finally end the inning.

The teams switched sides, and Red Sox Patsy Dougherty came to the plate. He struck out. The second hitter, Jimmy Collins, did the same. Chick Stahl managed to single to left, but he died on first when cleanup man Buck Freeman flied out to right.

Neither team scored in the second inning, but in

the third, the Pirates sweetened their lead by one on a single by Sebring that scored Bransfield. They added two more runs by the seventh inning; the second was the World Series' first home run, hit off of Sebring's talking bat.

With the score 7–0, a Pirates victory seemed all but certain. But Boston wasn't beaten yet. At the bottom of the seventh, Buck Freeman led off with a solid triple to right field. Freddy Parent followed with a triple of his own, scoring Freeman, and then crossed home plate himself on a sacrifice fly by Candy Lachance. The inning ended soon after that, but the Sox were finally on the scoreboard.

Boston added one more run in the ninth inning. But in the end, those three runs weren't enough. The Pirates won the first ever World Series game, 7–3.

Game two found Red Sox pitcher Bill Dinneen on the mound. He struck out the first batter. Eight and a half innings later, he'd struck out ten more and given up only three hits. Boston walked away with a 3–0 win — and the first World Series shutout — to tie the Series at one game apiece.

The next day, however, it was the Pirates' star pitcher, Deacon Phillippe, who led the charge, giving Pittsburgh a 4–2 victory over Boston. Phillippe pitched again in game four, the first played in Pittsburgh, and again, he was in top form, holding the Sox to just one run for the first eight innings. The Pirates, meanwhile, chalked up five.

Boston managed to push across three runs in the ninth and came very close to winning the game and tying the Series. But they didn't. Final score, 5–4 Pirates.

There were five games yet to be played in the best-of-nine series. The championship was still up for grabs.

The next game was scoreless through the fifth inning. Then, in the top of the sixth, the Red Sox loaded the bases. Pitcher William "Brickyard" Kennedy then handed Boston its first run by walking the next batter. Another run was scored when Wagner made a wild throw to first. Criger bunted in a third run, and two more runners crossed home plate when Young blasted a triple into the crowds in left field. When Dougherty also lambasted a triple, Young made it home. In a single inning, the score had gone from 0–0 to 6–0!

By the bottom of the ninth inning, the Red Sox had added five more, while the Pirates had posted a mere two runs for a final score of 11–2. The next day's game saw the Pirates falling again, this time 6–3. The Series was now tied at three games apiece.

Game seven was scheduled to be played the following afternoon in Pittsburgh. But Barney Dreyfuss postponed the game after receiving reports of sixty-mile-an-hour winds at Exposition Park. He believed that such winds could put the players at risk.

Boston players protested loudly. They thought that Dreyfuss had put off the game so that his team could recover from its two recent losses. If so, the strategy failed. Boston thrashed Pittsburgh 7–3 the next day.

The two teams returned to Boston for game eight. Once again, Bill Dinneen was masterful, sending the first eleven batters back to the dugout without a hit. He allowed Wagner a hit in the fourth inning, but Wagner died on base. Boston, meanwhile, racked up two runs that same inning, and then added another in the sixth.

The Pirates were still scoreless when they came to bat in the top of the ninth. The first two batters flied out, bringing up Wagner. Two pitches later, the count was 0 and 2.

A third strike would end the game and the Series. A hit would keep things alive for the Pirates. An article in the next day's *Boston Post* tells what happened next:

"Slowly [pitcher Bill Dinneen] gathered himself up for the effort, slowly he swung his arms above his head. Then the ball shot away like a flash toward the plate where the great Wagner stood, muscles drawn tense waiting for it. The big batsman's mighty shoulders heaved . . . as he swung his bat with every ounce of power in his body, but the dull thud of the ball, as it nestled in Criger's waiting mitt, told the story."

With that final strike, the Boston Red Sox won the first-ever World Series. There was no World Series in 1904 due to ongoing tension between the NL and the AL. But in 1905, the two organizations officially adopted the World Series as baseball's championship. That year, and the years that followed, the World Series saw play by some of the sport's best-known athletes. Cy Young, Honus Wagner, Ty Cobb,

Christy Mathewson, Rube Marquard, Frank Baker, Babe Adams, and their talented teammates all delivered outstanding performances that contributed to their teams' victories and helped the World Series become a world-class sporting event.

But even the most skilled athletes and teams have off days. The 1912 World Series proved that.

That year, the New York Giants faced the Boston Red Sox. The Giants had had a stellar year, with a final record of 103–48. The Sox were even better, posting 105 wins and 47 losses, a season record that went unmatched until 1931.

Strong pitching was a big reason for the two teams' successes. The Giants' Christy Mathewson won 23 games that season, and teammate Rube Marquard won 26, including an amazing 19 in a row. Rookie Jeff Tesreau led the league with an ERA of 1.96. Boston's staff wasn't as deep, but it boasted the rocket arm of twenty-two-year-old "Smokey Joe" Wood. Smokey Joe — who got his nickname after a teammate observed that his fastball "sure could smoke 'em!" — had won 34 games, 10 of which were shutouts.

Game one was played at the Polo Grounds in New York on October 8. Tesreau, jittery in front of such a large and vocal crowd, walked the first batter. Then he settled down and got the next three out. Smokey Joe retired the Giants without giving up a hit. The second inning went scoreless for both teams, too, but in the bottom of the third, Red Murray belted out a single that gave the Giants a 2–0 lead.

That's how the score stayed until the top of the sixth. Then, with one out and no one on base, Boston slugger Tris Speaker approached the plate. Tesreau toed the rubber and threw.

Crack! Speaker blasted a line drive to left center field.

Outfielder Fred Snodgrass moved to make the catch. So did Josh Devore. A moment later, Devore stepped aside. Snodgrass lifted his glove.

Bloop! The ball glanced off Snodgrass's glove and bounced away! What should have been an easy out was instead a stand-up triple. And when Duffy Lewis sent a grounder to second, Speaker raced home to give Boston its first run.

The Sox added three more runs in the top of the

seventh to go ahead 4–2. That was where the score remained until the bottom of the ninth.

Smokey Joe was still on the mound for Boston, but he was looking tired. He got one runner out but then gave up two singles and a double. With the score now 4–3 and runners on second and third, the Giants just needed a solid hit to take the game.

They didn't get it. Smokey Joe blasted his fastball by the next batter for his tenth strikeout of the game. He kept things tense by working the next batter, Doc Crandall, to a 3–2 count. Then, on the next pitch, Crandall swung — and missed. Wood had his eleventh strikeout and the Red Sox had their first win of the Series!

New York hoped to tie the Series in Boston the next day. But after going eleven innings, the match was called on account of darkness and ended in a 6–6 tie.

Darkness played a part in game three as well, but in a different way. The score was New York 2, Boston 1, in the bottom of the ninth. Boston had two outs and runners on second and third when Hick Cady socked a high fly ball into deep center field.

The runners on second and third charged home. The Sox won the game 3–2.

Or did they? What few people realized was that Josh Devore had caught Cady's hit for the game-ending third out! Devore had all but disappeared into darkness when he made the catch, and then, confident the out had been noted, he'd trotted off the field into the clubhouse. The final score was actually 2–1!

The Series was knotted at a game apiece. By the end of game three, it was 2–1 Boston, thanks to Smokey Joe and his eight strikeouts. Boston's lead was sweetened to 3–1 the following game, despite the best efforts of Christy Mathewson, who gave up only five hits. Those five were enough for the Sox to push across two runs, however, one better than the Giants.

But the next game, New York fought back and racked up five runs in the first inning! Although those were the only runs the Giants would get, they were enough to give them the victory.

Game six was played in Boston. As usual, the stands were full of Red Sox fans — too full, as it turned out. When the Royal Rooters, Boston's most faithful and intense fans, entered the park, they discovered that their usual seats were already occupied. Somehow, duplicate tickets had been sold.

The angry Rooters burst onto the field to protest. It took more than half an hour for order to be restored. During that time, Smokey Joe Wood sat on the bench. When the game finally started, his pitching arm was so cold that he gave up six runs in the first inning! The Giants took the game 11–4 to tie the Series at three games each.

The deciding game took place on Wednesday, October 16, at Fenway Park. Mathewson was pitching for the Giants. Hugh Bedient, a young but skilled pitcher, was on the mound for the Red Sox. The two had last battled in game five, with Bedient emerging as the winning pitcher. Whether he could best Mathewson again was anybody's guess.

Neither team scored in the first two innings. Then, in the third, Bedient walked leadoff batter Josh Devore, bringing up Red Murray. Murray blasted a drive toward left center field. Tris Speaker rushed back to make the catch but missed, putting the socre at Giants 1, Red Sox 0.

The Giants nearly scored again in the sixth inning,

when Larry Doyle slugged the ball to right center field. It looked like a surefire home run until outfielder Harry Hooper hurled himself over a low wall and snagged the ball out of the air.

The score was still 1–0 when Jake Stahl of the Red Sox came up to bat. There was one out. Stahl rapped a short fly ball to left center field. The Giants' shortstop, left fielder, and center fielder all headed toward it, gloves outstretched. But somehow, none of them made the catch! The ball fell to the ground, and Stahl was safe on second.

Mathewson appeared rattled by the flubbed play, for he walked the next batter to put runners at first and second. He worked pinch hitter Olaf Henriksen to a full count, and then threw a fadeaway pitch.

Pow! Henriksen connected with a searing blast past third base. Stahl scored and the game was tied.

The score was still 1–1 at the end of the ninth, forcing the game into extra innings.

The Giants took the lead in the top of the tenth, when Murray reached home after Speaker missed a pickup. The next batter, Chief Meyers, then blazed a line drive right at Wood, who had been brought in to help Boston to a win. Wood nabbed the ball with his pitching hand and threw Meyers out at first to end the inning.

Unfortunately, the catch injured Smokey Joe's hand. He took a seat on the bench and pinch hitter Clyde Engle took his turn at bat. Engle was a decent hitter, but not great. He connected for a floater toward center field, an easy out.

Fred Snodgrass held up his glove to catch the ball — and missed! Engle was safe at second.

Mathewson walked the next batter, Steve Yerkes. When Speaker popped up a foul between home and first, the second out — and possibly a game-ending double play — looked in the bag.

First baseman Fred Merkle, catcher Chief Meyers, and Mathewson all rushed for the catch. Merkle was closest, but for some reason, Mathewson bellowed for Meyers to take it. Meyers dove — and missed.

"That's gonna cost you this ball game!" Speaker yelled gleefully as he headed back to the plate. He backed up his bold words with a line drive to right. Engle scored, Yerkes went to third, and Speaker stood grinning at second. It was a tied game, and there were still two outs to go.

Mathewson walked the next batter to load the

bases. Then Larry Gardner came up to the plate with one intention in mind: to hit the ball far enough so that even if it was caught, Yerkes could tag up and beat the throw home.

Mathewson threw. Gardner connected. The ball flew toward right field. Devore got under it — and caught it!

Yerkes took off from third as if he'd been shot from a cannon. Devore hurled the ball to Meyers. Meyers stretched out his glove. The ball came fast, but Yerkes came faster. He hit the dirt in front of home plate and slid in under Meyers' glove! The Red Sox had their winning run — and their second World Series championship!

The *New York Times* would later report that the tenth inning of game eight was "the most stirring finish of a world championship in the history of baseball." Fortunately for baseball fans, there would be many more such finishes in the decades to come.

★ CHAPTER TWO ★

1920s

1924: The Big Train Steams to Victory

The Giants returned to the World Series in 1913, hoping this time to come out on top. They didn't. The Philadelphia Athletics beat them four games to one. The following year, the Boston Braves swept the A's in four straight games. The Red Sox, led by the pitching and batting skills of a young Babe Ruth, were victorious in 1915 and 1916, and again in 1918. In 1917, the White Sox took the championship away from the Giants. All these Series had memorable plays, but it was the 1919 World Series that found a place in the history books — for all the wrong reasons.

From 1914 to 1918, many countries, including the United States, were embroiled in World War I. Peace was finally declared at the end of 1918 and with it a return to life's normal routines. For many, that routine included baseball and the World Series.

That year, the Chicago White Sox were the heavy favorites to win the newly expanded, best-of-nine Series. Their opponents, the Cincinnati Reds, were a talented team but nowhere near as strong as the Sox. Yet to the amazement of many, the Chicago squad lost to Cincinnati, five games to three!

The reason for the stunning upset was revealed a year later. Several of the White Sox players, it turned out, had been paid by gamblers to throw the Series. The scandal rocked the baseball world; the disgraced players were banned from the sport and the team became forever known as the Black Sox.

Fortunately, the World Series of the early 1920s did much to restore baseball's good reputation. And in 1924, fans witnessed one of the best competitions the sport had yet seen.

"First in war, first in peace, last in the American League." That was the running joke about Washington, D.C., home of the United States government and the worst baseball team, the Washington Senators. Despite having one of the best hurlers in the game, Walter Johnson, the Senators had wound up in the cellar year after year. That changed at last in 1924, when Washington surprised everyone by beating out the mighty New York Yankees for a chance at the World Series title.

Their opponents were the other New York team, the Giants. The Giants had a formidable lineup including six batters who hit better than .300 that season. The Senators were the sentimental favorites, but against such competition, few believed they would come out on top.

Johnson, or the "Big Train," as he was known, pitched for the Senators in the opening game at Griffith Stadium in Washington. By the end of the ninth inning, he had struck out several batters — but he'd also given up two home runs. Luckily, Washington had managed to push two of their own runners across home plate. With the score 2–2, the game went into a tenth inning.

Then it went into an eleventh, and a twelfth. Johnson remained on the mound, but he was looking tired. He gave up two walks and three singles to hand the Giants two runs. The Senators added only one more in their last at bats.

The loss overshadowed the fact that Johnson had set a World Series record that day, striking out twelve batters. "I gave them everything I had, but it wasn't enough," he told a reporter, his voice laced with disappointment.

No one rooting for the Senators was disappointed by the second game, a 4–3 victory for Washington, although some may have wished the match hadn't been such a nail-biter. The Senators were up 3–0 in the fifth, saw their lead shrink by one in the sixth, and then disappear altogether when the Giants scored twice in the ninth.

Washington came up for their last raps with the score tied at 3–3. Leadoff batter Joe Judge walked and then was bunted to second. One out, but the game-winning run was in place.

The Senators' clutch man, Roger Peckinpaugh, faced pitcher Jack Bentley. He let the first pitch go by for a ball. He fouled the second to bring the count to one and one. And then he laced the next past the third baseman into the outfield. Judge charged from second to third and then flew the rest of the way home to make the score 4–3.

The Series score now stood at one game apiece.

Four games later, it stood at three games apiece. The 1924 World Series would be decided in the seventh and final game.

The game was played in Washington before a capacity crowd that included the president of the United States, Calvin Coolidge, and his wife, Grace. Grace Coolidge was an avid baseball fan. She and others in the crowd were undoubtedly puzzled when they saw who was on the pitcher's mound for the all-important game.

With a season record of 9–8, right-hander Curly Ogden was hardly the Senators' best pitcher. Why, then, was he starting when southpaw George Mogridge was available?

The reason had everything to do with strategy.

Statistically, left-handed batters do better against right-handed pitchers. The Giants had a powerful left-handed hitter, Bill Terry, who was averaging .500 in the Series. Once John McGraw, the Giants' manager, knew the Senators were starting a right-handed pitcher, he put Terry in the lineup.

That's what Bucky Harris, the Senators' manager and second baseman, was counting on. He allowed Ogden to pitch against two batters in the first inning. Then he pulled him from the game, put Mogridge in his place, and sat back to see what would happen when Mogridge faced Terry.

What happened was that Terry grounded out and struck out his first two at bats!

The game was scoreless until the bottom of the fourth. With one out and no one on base, Harris came to the plate. He smashed a long fly ball over the left-field fence for a home run! The Senators were on the scoreboard.

The score remained 1–0 until the top of the sixth. Pep Youngs walked and then advanced to third on a solid single from George Kelly's bat. Bill Terry was next in the roster. But McGraw pulled him and had a righty, Irish Meusel, pinch-hit against the lefty pitcher.

When Harris saw Meusel, he immediately took action. He replaced Mogridge with Firpo Marberry — a righty!

This time, however, the strategy failed to make a difference. Meusel hit deep into the outfield. The ball was caught for an out, but Pep Youngs tagged up and raced home to give the Giants their first run. Two batters later, they had their second — and they still had runners on first and second with only one out.

Grace Coolidge and the rest of the Senators' fans grew quiet. Would their beloved team bow down beneath the might of the Giants after all?

The answer seemed to be yes when New York added another run on a ball-between-the-legs error made by shortstop Ossie Bluege.

But Harris had one last card to play: Walter Johnson.

Few noticed Johnson warming up. They were too busy watching the action unfold on the field. Neither team scored in the seventh inning. Marberry held off the Giants in the top of the eighth. With the score 3–1, the Senators came up to bat.

Bluege, the first hitter, got out. Pinch hitter Nemo Leibold zinged a double into left field. Now Muddy Ruel approached the plate. Ruel hadn't gotten a hit the whole Series. This time, however, he singled. Leibold ran to third. The next batter, Bennie Tate, walked to load the bases.

The fans were on their feet, roaring for a hit. They didn't get one from Earl McNeely, who flied out. Two outs, bases loaded — and up came Bucky Harris. Harris took two strikes from pitcher Virgil Barnes. On the next, he laid down a grounder toward third.

Third baseman Fred Lindstrom moved forward.

As he crouched for the catch, the ball struck a small pebble and ricocheted into the air over his head!

That crazy hop gave Leibold and Ruel all the time they needed to race home. The inning ended soon after, but the Senators had tied the game at 3–3.

Now came the time for Bucky Harris to play his final card. When Walter Johnson walked out of the bull pen and onto the mound, the crowd erupted with cheers.

They cheered again when he retired the side without giving up a run. But the Senators didn't score in the ninth either. In fact, the score remained tied until the bottom of the twelfth inning.

Washington's first batter, Ralph Miller, grounded out to second. Then Ruel popped a high fly ball right over the plate.

New York's catcher, Hank Gowdy, tore off his mask and tracked the ball as it faded into the darkening sky and then started back down. Eye still on the ball, Gowdy lifted his glove and stepped back, right onto his mask! He lurched sideways and fell. The ball fell, too — right on the ground beside him.

Foul ball. Ruel, still alive, clocked a double off the next pitch.

With the winning run standing on second, Walter Johnson came up. He hit a bouncing grounder to short, a surefire out.

Or was it? Unbelievably, shortstop Travis Jackson kicked the ball — and Johnson arrived safely at first! He stayed there when the next batter, Earl McNeely, knocked a grounder to third. In a bizarre replay, the ball struck a pebble and took a wild hop over the third baseman's head — just as it had earlier in the game!

Ruel took off and ran as he had never run before. When he touched home plate, the crowd went insane. The Washington Senators, the worst team in the American League, had just stolen the World Series away from the mighty New York Giants!

"Winning today makes everything all right," Walter Johnson said later. "If I never pitch another ball game, I will have this one to remember, and I'll never forget it."

★ CHAPTER THREE ★

1930s

1932: The Legendary Called Shot

The most famous baseball player in the world is unquestionably George Herman "Babe" Ruth. The Babe debuted with the Red Sox in 1914. He spent five seasons in Boston, chalking up amazing stats and helping the team win the World Series in 1915, 1916, and 1918.

In 1920, he was traded to the New York Yankees. For the next fourteen seasons, he continued to astonish with his power at the plate and his prowess on the field. He also led the team to four World Series wins. While any World Series that featured the "Sultan of Swat" was exciting, one moment in the 1932 championship stands out as the most memorable — and the most controversial — in baseball history.

New York faced the Chicago Cubs that year. Animosity between the two clubs was running high even before the Series began. Why? Midseason, Chicago had acquired a new shortstop, Mark Koenig, from New York. The former Yankee went on to bat .353 in the thirty-three games he played as a Cub. In New York's opinion, Koenig was a big reason the Cubs had reached the World Series. When they found out Chicago planned to give Koenig only a half-share of any World Series winnings, they were outraged for their old teammate — and announced their outrage publicly.

New York's manager, Joe McCarthy, also had a grudge against Chicago. Two years earlier, he had been fired as manager of the Cubs when the team failed to repeat as pennant winners. Now, he wanted nothing more than to show them what they had given up by beating them in the Series.

The first game took place on September 28 at Yankee Stadium. Besides Babe Ruth, the Yankees had the might of their star first baseman, Lou Gehrig. Together, the two sluggers had a combined total of 75 home runs for the regular season. Many New York fans hoped to see one or both of them add to that total that day.

Getting hits, let alone homers, off the Cubs would

be difficult, however, for Chicago had a very strong pitching staff. Lon Warneke boasted a 2.37 ERA that year and accounted for 22 of the team's 90 wins; Guy Bush added another 19, and Charlie Root 15. The Cubs also had an impressive lineup of hitters, including future Hall-of-Famers Billy Herman, Gabby Hartnett, and Kiki Cuyler, whose triple on September 20 had clinched the NL pennant for the Cubs.

The Cubs got on the scoreboard first. First Billy Herman singled to center field. Then Woody English clocked a hit into right. It could have been an out, but the Babe bobbled the play. Herman flew around the bases and made it home. English, meanwhile, stood safe at third. Two batters later, he, too, raced home. The inning ended soon after, but the Yankees were already in the hole by two runs!

Three innings later, they were still down by two. In fact, they hadn't even managed to get a hit off pitcher Guy Bush! Then, in the fourth inning, their bats finally came alive. Ruth singled, scoring Earle Combs, whom Bush had sent to first on a walk. Then, with Ruth at first, Gehrig blasted a home run. The inning ended with the score 3–2 in New York's favor.

It stayed that way until the bottom of the sixth inning. Bush was still on the mound, but when he walked the first three batters to load the bases, it was obvious he was tired. Still, the Cubs' manager kept him in — a move that proved to be a mistake. When Bush was finally relieved four batters later, the score had jumped from 3–2 to 6–2. And it didn't stop there. The Yankees added two more runs before the Cubs finally ended the inning.

A six-run deficit is difficult, but not impossible, to overcome. Chicago managed to inch two runs closer in the seventh inning. But New York had a full head of steam going and at the bottom of the same inning added five more to their side. The two final runs Chicago posted the next inning simply weren't enough. New York took the win with a final tally of twelve runs to Chicago's six.

The Cubs got off to a quick start with a run their first at bat the next day. But New York answered right back, pushing two runners across. Chicago rallied in the third to tie things up 2–2, but the tie didn't last long. The bottom of that same inning, both Ruth and Gehrig crossed home plate to make it 4–2 Yankees. Two innings later, they added the fifth and final run of the game to go ahead by two in the Series.

The third game took place in Chicago. The stands were crammed with Cubs fans desperate for a home-team victory. Hoping to distract or anger the Yankee players, they jeered, stomped their feet, and yelled insults at them. The Chicago dugout was just as loud, taking every opportunity to bad-mouth New York's players.

New York seemed unfazed by the taunts; in fact, they gave as good as they got, and then did much to silence the noise with their playing.

Earle Combs, the first Yankee batter, came up to the plate and made it to second on an error by the Cubs' shortstop. The next batter, Joe Sewell, walked. Runners were now on first and second.

Now Babe Ruth strode to the plate. The yelling from the stands and Chicago's dugout grew deafening. It ended abruptly, however, when Ruth clobbered a home run!

The three-run lead shrank to two when the Cubs scored their first turn at bat. By the fifth inning, the game was tied at four runs apiece.

Once again, the Sultan of Swat approached the

plate amidst a raucous roar. He stepped into the batter's box and eyed pitcher Charlie Root.

Root reared back and threw. Ruth let it go by.

"Strike one!" the umpire called.

Root got the ball back from catcher Gabby Hartnett, took the signal, and hurled again. Ball one.

The third pitch was also a ball. Ruth watched the fourth go by for a second called strike. He lifted his hand in the air to acknowledge the umpire's call. Then he pointed his finger.

That finger point has become one of baseball's most controversial and enduring legends. It is controversial because no one can agree what Ruth was really pointing at. Some believe he was jabbing his finger at the loudmouthed players in the Cubs' dugout. Others think his single raised finger was saying he only needed one more pitch to get a hit.

But the most popular explanation says that the Babe pointed his finger at the center-field stands, as if to say that's where he was going to hit the ball. And when he socked Root's next pitch into those very stands, his finger point became known forever more as the "called shot."

No one will ever truly know what Babe Ruth

meant, however, because he never said. He simply rounded the bases with a broad smile on his face.

Ruth's blast is perhaps the most famous home run of all time. But it wasn't the last one of that game. Gehrig followed with his second homer immediately after, lofting the Yankees score to 7–5 for their third straight win of the Series.

Game four was also held in Chicago. Before the game, baseball commissioner Kenesaw Mountain Landis issued an order to both clubs — behave like civilized human beings or else. The two teams obeyed.

Of course, the fans hadn't been given any such order. They were as rowdy as ever when their home team took the field. Their enthusiasm fizzled, however, when the Yankees chalked up a run in the first inning. But it rose again to a fever pitch before the inning was over, because Chicago put across four runs!

The score remained 4–1 through the second inning. Then New York added two more runs, including a homer, in the third. The Cubs couldn't answer their turn at bat — in fact, by the top of the ninth, Chicago's bats seemed to have lost their voices almost completely.

The Yankees' wood, meanwhile, was screaming.

By the game's end, the score stood at 13–6! New York had completely silenced the raucous Chicago team by sweeping them from the Series in four straight games. The Yankees returned home as heroes while the Cubs licked their wounds.

The Cubs made it back to the Series again in 1935, only to lose to the Detroit Tigers two games to four. New York beat them again in 1938. But by then, winning the championship had become something of a habit for the Yankees. From 1936 to 1946, they reached the World Series seven times and won the title six times!

They won an eighth ticket to the Series again in 1947. This was an amazing achievement, yet something else even more amazing happened that year — something that changed baseball forever.

★ CHAPTER FOUR ★

1940s

1947: Seventh-Game Showdown

By the start of the 1947 season, professional baseball was several decades old. During those years, leagues had formed and disbanded. Players and teams had survived two World Wars. Rules and equipment had changed the way the game was played. And the World Series had gone from a little-watched event to the most popular championship in the nation.

But one thing had remained consistent throughout these years: every player in the National League and the American League was white. An unspoken agreement amongst the team owners had seen to that.

That finally changed in 1947, when the Brooklyn Dodgers signed an African-American player named Jackie Robinson. Robinson was an outstanding athlete who also possessed the inner strength to withstand the prejudice he encountered. Rather than get angry, he let his fleet feet, powerful hitting, quick glove, and rocket arm speak for him. Thanks to his fortitude, baseball's color barrier was finally being broken.

It was also thanks to Robinson — at least in part — that the Dodgers won the NL pennant in 1947. They had last been to the World Series in 1941, when they had lost to the Yankees four games to one. Now the Dodgers had a chance to even the score, for the Yankees were going to the Series again. The question was, did the Brooklyn team have the muscle to overthrow their awesome opponents?

On paper, the Yankees were the stronger club. They had a season record of 97 wins and 57 losses, with 115 home runs and 1,439 hits. Offensively, they had racked up 794 runs while allowing their opponents only 568. Brooklyn, on the other hand, had a season record of 94–60. They had 11 fewer hits than the Yankees, and of their 774 runs, only 83 were homers.

The 1947 Subway Series opened on September 30 in Yankee Stadium before a capacity crowd that included such baseball dignitaries as Babe Ruth, Ty

Cobb, and Cy Young. Rookie pitcher Francis Joseph Shea, better known as "Spec" because of his freckles, jogged out to the mound for the Yankees. He got the Dodgers' first batter, Eddie Stanky, to fly out.

Now Jackie Robinson stepped into the batter's box. Six pitches later, he had a free ticket to first base. He tossed the bat aside and trotted down the line amidst thunderous applause. Moments later, he stole second. But he didn't stay there for long. When Dodger Dixie Walker singled into left, Robinson dashed past third on his way to home — and into the history books as the first African-American to score a run in the World Series.

That was Brooklyn's only run that inning, but their pitcher, Ralph Branca, held their lead by retiring the first three Yankees in order. Amazingly, he did the same thing again in the second inning — and the third, and the fourth!

Branca's perfect game came to an end in the fifth. First Joe DiMaggio clubbed a grounder between short and third that landed him safely at first. That single was followed by two walks. With the bases loaded and no outs, the next batter, Johnny Lindell, socked a double behind third base. Two runs had been scored and there were still no outs. Then Phil Rizzuto walked, and the bases were loaded again!

After four no-hit innings, Branca was suddenly falling apart. The Dodgers' manager pulled him from the game. Now it was up to reliever Hank Behrman to shut down the Yankees.

But Behrman handed New York another run when he walked the batter he faced. Before the inning was over, the score had jumped from 1–0 to 5–1. Although Brooklyn managed to add two runs, it wasn't enough. New York took the game, 5–3.

The next day, the Yankees lit up four Brooklyn pitchers for fifteen hits, including three triples and a home run. Defensively, the Dodgers looked like rank amateurs. They dropped balls, overran easy grounders, and threw wildly. When the dust finally settled, the Yankees had ten runs. Brooklyn had only three — and by all accounts, they were lucky to have gotten them.

Game three, however, the Dodgers drew first blood, scoring six runs in the second inning! New York managed to cough up a pair during their turn at bat but then saw the Dodgers pull further ahead with yet another run in the bottom of the third. Going into the fourth inning, it was Brooklyn 7, New York 2.

The Yankees roared back to draw within two, and then within one. With the score teetering at 9–8 at the top of the ninth, their momentum slowed and finally stopped. The Dodgers retired the side one-two-three to win game three.

Anyone who left game four after eight innings the next night undoubtedly believed New York had added another win to their side. But they were wrong — and they missed one of the most exciting endings of any World Series game yet.

Going into the bottom of the ninth, the score was Yankees 2, Dodgers 1. Brooklyn hadn't taken the lead once that game; it seemed doubtful they would take it in their last raps. But, as Yankee Yogi Berra would one day observe, "It ain't over 'til it's over" — and New York still needed to get three outs before it was over for Brooklyn.

They got one when Brooklyn's first batter hit a long fly ball to left field that Johnny Lindell caught near the wall. Pitcher Bill Bevens walked the next batter, Carl Furillo. Furillo was not known for his speed, so the Dodgers had fleet-footed Al Gion-friddo run for him.

Gionfriddo waited at second while the next batter fouled out. With two outs and only one man on, the Dodgers needed a hit — badly.

Manager Burt Shotton had a choice. He could have pitcher Hugh Casey hit. Or he could have Pete Reiser pinch-hit. Usually he wouldn't have hesitated to put in Reiser. But Reiser had injured his ankle the previous game. Unless he really belted the ball in just the right spot, there was little chance he would be able to outrun a throw to first.

Shotton decided to risk it. He also risked giving Gionfriddo the steal sign. Both risks paid off. Gion-friddo slid under Phil Rizzuto's throw, landing safely at second, and Bevens intentionally walked Reiser. There were runners at first and second, and two outs.

So far, the Yankees hadn't given up a single hit in the game; the Dodgers' one run had come on walks and an error. If they got the next batter out, New York would be the first team to win a no-hitter in the World Series.

Of course, that was the last thing Brooklyn wanted.

Shotton sent pinch hitter Cookie Lavagetto to the plate with one order: Get a hit.

Lavagetto obeyed. On the second pitch, he blasted the ball far into the right field toward the concrete wall. He took off for first. Eddie Miksis, running for Reiser, dashed for second. Gionfriddo ran for third.

Meanwhile, outfielder Tommy Henrich was fading back. He had a choice: jump up against the wall to try to make the game-ending catch or pick up the ball after it hit the dirt and hope he could throw out a runner before the winning run was scored.

With a history-making no-hit game on the line, he went for the catch — only realizing seconds later that the catch was impossible to make. The ball ricocheted off the concrete at a crazy angle. By the time Henrich got his hands on it, not one but *two* runners had touched home plate. The Dodgers won the game, 3–2!

The Series now stood at two games each. It was still tied after the next two meetings. That sixth game, a Brooklyn win, was memorable for one truly remarkable play.

It was 8–5 at the bottom of the sixth. The first

Yankee batter got out on a line drive, the second got a free ticket to first, the third popped out into foul territory, and the fourth got a single. That brought up New York's finest, Joe DiMaggio. With two men on, two men out, he needed a hit.

He connected on southpaw reliever Joe Hatten's first pitch. The ball soared into the left field near the bull pen. The runners took off and crossed home plate. DiMaggio rounded first at full speed and then, certain his hit was a home run, slowed to a jog.

Outfielder Al Gionfriddo wasn't jogging, however. He was sprinting. When that fly ball came down, he was there to make the catch. And what a catch it was — a beautiful, over-the-shoulder, top-of-the-wall, one-handed nab that robbed DiMaggio of his homer, erased the two runs, and ended the inning with the Dodgers still ahead by three! And when the game ended with Brooklyn still up by two, the 1947 World Series was forced into the seventh and final game.

The Dodgers were still riding high when they entered Yankee Stadium for the last game. In the second inning, they knocked in two runs.

Unfortunately for Brooklyn fans, those two runs were all the Dodgers would get. New York answered with a run in the second, and then added two more in the fourth, one in the sixth, and one in the seventh. The game, and the Series, ended in the top of the ninth with a classic, shortstop-to-second-to-first double play.

The Dodgers had lasted longer against the Yankees than anyone had expected. But in the end, the Yankees were simply too powerful, that year and in the years to come. The two teams battled for the championship title several more times in the next decade, but only once did the Dodgers come out on top.

★ CHAPTER FIVE ★

1950s

1955: The Dynasty Is Toppled — Once

Baseball in the 1950s was dominated by one team: the New York Yankees. From 1950 to 1959, they earned trips to the World Series an amazing eight times, winning seven. Three of those wins came after they beat the Brooklyn Dodgers. But in 1955, it was the Dodgers who at last bested their archrivals.

The 1954 Series was one of the two series not to feature the Yankees. That year, the other New York team, the Giants, pounded the Cleveland Indians four games to none. But the 1954 World Series isn't remembered for that sweep; it's remembered for what is now simply called "the Catch."

The New York Giants had several strong players on their team, but their star player was twenty-three-year-old center fielder Willie "Say Hey Kid"

Mays. Powered by his batting and fielding skills, the team won 97 games that year.

In game one of the Series, he proved just how good he was. It was the top of the eighth inning. The score was tied 3–3. The Indians had runners at first and second, no outs, when their slugger, Vic Wertz, came to the plate. Wertz was three-for-three so far, including a first-inning triple that scored the team's first two runs. No doubt he believed he'd added a fourth hit when he socked relief pitcher Don Liddle's first pitch into deep center field. In fact, he and everyone else in the stadium believed he'd just hit a home run.

Everyone, that is, except Willie Mays. The moment Wertz connected, the fleet-footed outfielder turned his back on home plate and ran. The outfield fence at the Polo Grounds in New York is 460 feet from home plate. Wertz's blast looked certain to clear it before Mays could get there.

But unbelievably, Mays did get there! His back still to the plate, he reached up and snagged the ball out of the air. Instead of a home run, Wertz was out!

Mays didn't stop to congratulate himself, however. He knew those two runners could tag up and head home. So he whirled around and whipped the ball in, holding the runners on base. His speed, powerful throwing arm, and lightning-quick reflexes kept the Indians from earning three runs.

"I had it the whole time," Mays joked later. Spurred on by his remarkable catch, the Giants took the game and, three days later, the Series.

The following postseason saw the Dodgers and the Yankees meeting for their sixth Subway Series. Brooklyn was the sentimental favorite; some baseball fans, including New York followers, were simply tired of seeing the Yankees win.

Game one was played at Yankee Stadium before a crowd of nearly 64,000 people. After a hitless first inning, both teams posted a pair of runs in the second and added one more each in the third to make the score 3–3 going into the fourth.

By the sixth inning, however, the Yankees had pushed across three more, two of which were home runs by first baseman Joe Collins. But the Dodgers weren't finished yet.

At the top of the eighth inning, Dodger Carl Furillo singled, stood on first while Gil Hodges got out, and then advanced to third when the third baseman flubbed Jackie Robinson's hit. Robinson reached second on that error. The next batter hit a sacrifice fly for the second out, but Furillo made it home and Robinson was at third.

In his heyday, Robinson had been notorious for stealing bases. But now, few believed the thirty-six-year-old veteran was the threat he had once been. Certainly pitcher Whitey Ford didn't think he was worth worrying about. He prepared to face the next batter with scarcely a glance at Robinson.

That was a mistake. The moment Ford went into his windup, Robinson took off. He was attempting to steal home!

The crowd went wild. Catcher Yogi Berra shouted to Ford. Ford threw. Berra stood to make the play. Robinson hit the dirt and slid feet-first toward home plate. Amidst a cloud of dust, Berra caught the ball, fell to his knees, and tagged Robinson.

Both men froze and looked at the umpire. Time seemed to stand still. Then the umpire made his call.

"Safe!"

Jackie Robinson had stolen home! The Dodgers were within one run of tying the Yankees!

Unfortunately for Brooklyn, they were still one

run behind when the game ended. They dropped the next game, too, giving New York a two-game lead in the Series. But in game three, the Dodgers proved they weren't pushovers — and Robinson proved that he still had a few tricks up his sleeve.

At the bottom of the seventh, Brooklyn was ahead 6–3. But Robinson knew that that three-run lead could vanish in an instant. He decided to sweeten it if he could. After Gil Hodges flied out to left field, Robinson came up to bat. He hit a solid blast down the left-field line. He stretched the hit into a double, touching the base as he ran past it and then turning to jog back to the bag.

Outfielder Elston Howard nabbed the ball from the ground and then glanced at Robinson. He thought Robinson was too far off the bag. One quick throw, and he could get Robinson out.

However, Robinson was one step ahead of him — literally. When Howard hurled the ball to second, Robinson whirled back around and charged to third, beating the relay throw! Robinson was safe, and when Sandy Amoros hit a single to right, he made it home to put the Dodgers up 7–3. It was a trick he'd used many times early in his career, but one that no one had expected to see him pull the World Series!

Brooklyn added another run that inning and went on to win, 8–3. Totally juiced by their victory, they took the next two games to go ahead in the Series.

Then New York tied it all up in game six, forcing the championship to a final meeting. The Dodgers and the Yankees had been in this same situation in 1947 and in 1952. Both times the Yankees had won the seventh game.

Game seven was bittersweet for Robinson. Having aggravated an old injury to his heel, he was forced to watch the action unfold from the sidelines. Still, he had a front-row seat to the deciding match — and what a match it was.

On the mound for the Dodgers was rookie pitcher Johnny Podres. Inning after inning, Podres defused every Yankee threat, denying them a place on the scoreboard. Brooklyn, on the other hand, chalked up two runs. When Elston Howard grounded out in the ninth inning, Podres' shutout was complete — and the Dodgers had finally beaten the Yankees to become World Champions!

Unfortunately for Brooklyn fans, it was the last time the Dodgers would come out on top in the Subway Series. New York beat them in seven games the following year, and in 1958 the Brooklyn franchise was moved to Los Angeles, ending the cross-city rivalry forever.

It wasn't the end of the Yankees' reign, however. Far from it.

★ CHAPTER SIX ★

1960s

1960: The Pirates Steal the Series

The Pittsburgh Pirates and the New York Yankees had last met for the World Series in 1927. Then, the Pirates collapsed beneath the might of the Yankees, losing in four straight games. Their defeat had been handed to them in part by a pair of New York sluggers, Babe Ruth and Lou Gehrig.

Now, thirty-three years later, history seemed about to repeat itself. New York had powered its way to its eleventh American League pennant thanks to its two home-run kings, Mickey Mantle and Roger Maris. Together, Maris and "the Mick" accounted for 79 of the Yankees' 193 home runs in 1960. Going into the Series, New York looked unstoppable — none of the teams they had faced in their last fifteen regular-season games had been able to stop them, anyway.

But the Pirates were no slouches either. Their

record of 95–59 was nearly even with New York's 97–57.

Still, most baseball followers didn't think Pittsburgh stood a chance against New York. The Yankees had been world champions eighteen times. The Pirates hadn't even won a pennant in more than three decades.

At first, they seemed correct, for the leadoff batter, Yankee Tony Kubek, knocked out a single. But then Hector Lopez hit into a double play and the threat was defused, at least for the moment.

Then Roger Maris came to the plate. He did just what Yankee fans hoped he would do — he clobbered a home run. Then cleanup hitter Mickey Mantle made the third out.

Art Ditmar was on the mound for New York. He faced six batters and gave up a walk, a double, and three singles, to hand the Pirates three runs and only one out!

Five hits, three runs? Manager Casey Stengel yanked Ditmar before any more damage was done. Ditmar's replacement, Jim Coates, retired the next two batters to end the painful inning.

By the top of the ninth, the Pirates had jumped ahead 6–2. Four runs is a comfortable lead but not insurmountable, especially for a team as powerful as the Yankees. Their first hitter, Gil McDougald, belted out a solid single. A minute later, however, he trotted back to the dugout after being forced out at second. Bobby Richardson was still on first, though. Then Elston Howard blasted a home run! Suddenly, Pittsburgh's four-run lead had narrowed to two — and when Tony Kubek singled, it seemed possible that the Yankees could steal the game from the Pirates.

They didn't. Despite being outhit 13 to 8, Pittsburgh won, 6–4.

The next day, Pirates fans flocked to the stadium, hoping to see their team go up by two. Instead, they watched New York ring the home team's bell to the tune of sixteen runs, two of which were classic Mantle homers. And the third game was even worse — Yankee pitcher Whitey Ford allowed the Pirates only four hits and no runs while New York racked up sixteen hits for ten runs to go ahead in the Series two games to one.

Amazingly, Pittsburgh squeaked out a 3–2 win in

game four to tie the Series. Then they outhit the Yankees the next day on their way to a 5–2 win and their first Series lead.

Whitey Ford was back on the mound for game six. He confounded the Pirates' batters again to earn his second shutout of the Series. The Yankees, meanwhile, crossed home plate twelve times! With the score at three games each, the Series was going into a seventh deciding game.

Statistically, the Series seemed weighted in the Yankees' favor. They had a six-game total of 46 runs; the Pirates had 17. The Yankees had 78 hits; the Pirates had 42. The Yankees had eight home runs; the Pirates had one. The Yankees had shut out the Pirates twice; in both those games, the Pirates had allowed the Yankees to get into the double digits.

Yet if the Pirates went into game seven feeling demoralized, they didn't show it. They scored four runs while holding the Yankees scoreless. In fact, New York didn't get on the board until the top of the fifth, and then only for one run.

Then came the sixth inning. After all but shutting down the New York offense, pitcher Vern Law gave up a single and a walk before being relieved by Roy Face.

But Face fared no better. While Maris fouled out, Mantle singled, scoring Bobby Richardson and sending Tony Kubek to third. Then Yogi Berra clocked a three-run homer. Suddenly, the Pirates were in the hole, 5–4!

The score was still 5–4 at the top of the eighth. Face retired New York's biggest threats, Maris and Mantle — only to walk Berra, give up singles to Bill Skowron and Johnny Blanchard, and then a double to Clete Boyer! The score leaped from a manageable 5–4 to an unwieldy 7–4 before the inning finally ended.

Pittsburgh fans at Forbes Field slumped in their seats. Their team had just two at bats to overcome a three-run lead. Given their hitting stats, two didn't seem nearly enough.

First up in the bottom of the eighth was pinch hitter Gino Cimoli. He tapped out a single. Then Bill Virdon plugged a grounder right toward shortstop Tony Kubek.

Kubek crouched for the easy catch. *Thock!* The

ball struck something in the grass and ricocheted right into Kubek's neck! As Kubek lay in the dirt, clutching his injury, Cimoli charged to second and Virdon reached first.

Two men on, no outs? Pittsburgh fans sat up a little straighter.

The third batter, Dick Groat, singled to score Cimoli and send Virdon to second. The score was now 7–5. There were still no outs and runners on first and second. One sacrifice bunt later, those runners had advanced to second and third. One good hit could score Virdon; a great hit could tie the game.

But the next batter, Rocky Nelson, flied out. That brought up right fielder Roberto Clemente. Clemente did what Nelson hadn't been able to do, namely, rap out a single to score Virdon.

Pirate fans leaped to their feet with a roar. The home team was within one of tying the game!

Now Hal Smith came up. Smith was a solid player but not a top hitter. No one expected him to provide the run they needed.

Yet Smith did provide — and how! When reliever Jim Coates delivered his pitch, Smith blasted the

THE **BOSTON RED SOX** 1918

LAWLER MILLER JONES THOMAS RUTH HOOPER MAYS SHEAN KINNEY STRUNK McINNIS BARROW
SCOTT DUBUC BUSH WHITEMAN SCHANG MAYER WAGNER AGNEW COFFEY
MASCOT & BATBOY

The 1918 Boston Red Sox team photo (Babe Ruth second row, fourth from left). Ruth pitched the team to their fourth World Series win of the decade.

Lou Gehrig crosses home, thanks to a two-run homer by Babe Ruth in the New York Yankees 1932 World Series victory.

"The Catch," made by Willie Mays during the 1954 World Series.

Bill "Maz" Mazeroski comes home after hitting the first ever Series-winning homer in 1960.

Carlton Fisk waves his arms, willing his blast during the 1975 World Series to drop fair. The ball struck the foul pole for a home run.

AP/Wide World Photos

In 1977, Reggie Jackson does what only one other player—Babe Ruth—had ever done before: hit three consecutive homers in one game in the World Series.

Kirk Gibson, sidelined with painful injuries, came off the bench to hit a two-run, game-winning homer in the 1988 World Series.

The Boston Red Sox reverse the 86-year-old "Curse of the Bambino" by winning the 2004 World Series.

ball deep for a three-run homer! The slugfest ended with the next batter, but the Pirates were once again ahead, 9–7.

There was still one inning left, however, and the Yankees used their turn at bat to full advantage. The first batters singled. Roger Maris popped a foul ball for the first out, but the threat of two runners on base still remained. Mickey Mantle made good on the threat by singling one runner home. They needed only one more to tie things up. They got it in classic fashion.

Yogi Berra was up. He drove the ball down the first-base line. Mantle, at first, started for second just as first baseman Rocky Nelson gloved the ball and stepped on the bag. Berra was out — and Mantle would have been, too, if Nelson had managed to tag him before he returned to first base. But he didn't. Mantle dove for the bag and slid under Nelson's glove a split second before the tag.

And meanwhile, the runner on third had taken off for home. When he scored, the game was tied at 9 apiece.

That's how the score remained when the Pirates came up in the bottom of the ninth. If they could push across just one run, they would beat the seemingly unbeatable Yankees. If they didn't, the game would go into extra innings. That, they knew, could very well prove disastrous for them.

Leading off for Pittsburgh was Bill Mazeroski. "Maz," as he was known, had had a strong Series so far, including a two-run homer in game one. He]stood at the plate, facing reliever Ralph Terry. Terry's first pitch was high. Maz let it go by for ball one. The second pitch was also high. This time, however, Maz swung — hard.

Boom!

The sound of bat hitting ball echoed around the stadium for a microsecond before being drowned out by the roar of the crowd. It was a home run, the first World Series–winning homer ever!

Maz rounded the bases waving his cap and grinning ear to ear. Pittsburgh fans jumped, screamed, and danced in the stands. Sure, the Yankees had beaten them in stats — outhitting, outfielding, and outpitching the Pirates in nearly every game — but in the end, the only stat that mattered was the final score of the final game. And thanks to Maz, that score was Pittsburgh 10, New York 9. The Pirates were world champs for the first time since 1925.

Unfortunately for Pirates fans, the decade would end without Pittsburgh reaching the Series again. New York returned for the next four years, winning back-to-back championships in 1961 and 1962, but then losing it twice in a row.

★ CHAPTER SEVEN ★

1970s

1975: The Best Sixth Game Ever

After their second straight World Series loss in 1964, the Yankees' star finally began to fade. The team that had won nineteen World Series since 1923 wouldn't return to the big game until the next decade. During their absence, other teams rose to greatness. The most notable being the Oakland Athletics. The A's were "three-peat" champs in 1972, 1973, and 1974, making them the second team in Major League history to win more than two in a row.

In 1975, however, two other teams took the field to battle for the championship. And by all accounts, that Series was one of the most memorable in baseball history.

That year, the Cincinnati Reds were the dominant team in the National League. The "Big Red Machine," as they were known, was powered by Pete

Rose, Ken Griffey Sr., Johnny Bench, and Dave Concepcion, among others. They crushed the opposition, winning 108 times while losing only 54. In the postseason, they swept the Pittsburgh Pirates in three straight games and entered the World Series hungry for victory.

But their competition was equally hungry — and almost as strong as the Reds. The Boston Red Sox had ended with a 95–65 record thanks to the might of rookie sluggers Jim Rice and Fred Lynn as well as veterans Dwight Evans, Carl "Yaz" Yastrzemski, Luis Tiant, and Carlton Fisk. They, too, swept their opponents in the playoffs. If they won this World Series, it would be their first since Babe Ruth pitched for them in 1918.

Game one took place on October 11 at Fenway Park. Inning after inning passed without a run. The score was still zero to zero when the Sox came up to bat at the bottom of the seventh.

First up was pitcher Luis Tiant. He hadn't come up to bat in the last three regular seasons. But World Series rules state that all pitchers must hit and surprisingly, Tiant connected for a single into left field.

That brought up Dwight Evans, who laid down a

bunt toward the pitcher's mound. The pitcher fielded the ball cleanly, turned to throw out Tiant at second, and slipped! By the time he'd recovered, Tiant and Evans were safe on base.

The next batter bounced the ball between third and short for a single. Bases loaded, no outs — and power hitter Yaz was on his way to the plate. Things did not look good for the Reds.

A minute later, they looked even worse. Yaz stroked a single to right. Tiant took a trip home, missed the plate, but returned to tag it to give the Sox the first run of the game.

Two pitchers and two innings later, the 0–0 deadlock had turned into a 6–0 blowout for the Sox. Tiant walked off the field with a complete-game, five-hit shutout under his belt.

The Reds tied the Series the next day, vaulting over the Red Sox with two runs late in the game.

Game three looked good for the Reds, who led 5–2 after six innings. But one run at a time, the Sox whittled away the Reds' lead until they'd tied things up and forced the game into extra innings. They came close to going up in the top of the tenth, when

Yaz clocked the ball to deep center field. But River-front Stadium has plenty of room for fielders to chase down balls, and that's just what center fielder Cesar Geronimo did. Yaz was out, and when Fisk hit into a double play, the inning ended with the score still tied.

Geronimo helped the Reds again by leading off with a single to right. Pinch hitter Ed Armbrister came up next with instructions to bunt.

What followed was a confusing and controversial baseball moment. Armbrister bunted the ball into the dirt right in front of home plate. A split second later, the umpire called it fair.

Catcher Carlton Fisk darted forward to nab the ball. As he did, he collided with Armbrister. After they separated, Armbrister headed for first and Fisk threw to second, hoping to get Geronimo out.

But his throw was wild — so wild, in fact, that Armbrister made it all the way to second and Geronimo stood safe at third!

Sox manager Darrell Johnson raced out of the dugout to protest. According to baseball rules, any runner who interferes with a fielder trying to make a play on a batted ball is automatically out, even if the interference is not intentional. Armbrister had interfered with Fisk and was therefore out — or so it seemed to Johnson, the rest of the Sox, and many others who'd seen the play.

But the umpire stood by his call. When the Reds pushed across the game-winning run three batters later, the Sox stormed off the field, furious.

They channeled that fury the next day, beating the Reds 5–4. But game five belonged to the Reds, thanks to two powerful home runs from Tony Perez's bat.

Like most World Series, this championship had provided plenty of excitement. But game six made every other match look dull in comparison.

After a three-day rain delay, Luis Tiant took the mound. He retired the first three Reds in order. Then, in the Red Sox's first at bats, Fred Lynn lambasted a three-run homer.

The score stayed 3–0 until the top of the fifth, when the Reds scored twice on a triple by Griffey, and then again on a single by Bench.

Two innings later, the Reds added two to their

side. They added yet another in the eighth with a home run by Geronimo.

The Sox came up in the bottom of the eighth with the score 6–3. Lynn singled and Rico Petrocelli walked to put runners at first and second, no outs. Bernie Carbo came in to pinch-hit for pitcher Roger Moret. It was Carbo's first at bat of the game. He took two strikes and then connected weakly for a foul ball. One more strike and the inning would be over.

That strike didn't come. Instead, Carbo absolutely crushed the next pitch, blasting the ball deep into home-run territory to tie the game!

The score was still 6–6 after nine innings. And after ten innings. And after eleven — although the Reds came very close to winning the game that inning. With Ken Griffey at first, slugger Joe Morgan slammed a sizzling line drive down the right-field line. Griffey took off, certain that the hit was unreachable.

But nobody told Dwight Evans that. He beat the ball to the wall, nabbed it in the webbing of his glove as he crashed into the concrete, and then threw to first for the double play!

With the clock ticking past midnight, the game continued into a twelfth inning. But no one watching the game was yawning; it was simply too suspenseful!

Bottom of the twelfth, the score was still tied. As leadoff batter Fisk readied himself in the on-deck circle, he turned to Fred Lynn and said, "I'm gonna hit one off the wall. You drive me in."

Lynn answered, "Sounds good to me."

Fisk stepped into the batter's box. He let the first pitch go by for ball one. The next pitch would have been a strike if Fisk had let it go by or had swung and missed. But he did neither. Instead, he connected.

Boom! The ball soared high in the air toward the left-field line and vanished into the outfield lights. Fisk tracked the ball's flight, and then began hopping and chopping his arms sideways toward right field, willing the ball to stay fair of the foul pole.

Clang! The ball hit the pole square on! Home run! Red Sox fans swarmed the field as Fisk frisked around the bases. When he reached home, he gave a final jump and came down on the plate with both feet.

"I don't think I've ever gone through a more emotional game," Fisk told reporters later.

Sadly for Boston fans, the Red Sox couldn't follow up that amazing win with another the following night. After leading the game 3–2 through six innings, Boston gave up two runs without being able to score any more of their own. The Series outcome didn't come as a surprise to anyone who relied on statistics to predict the winner — after all, the Reds were the strongest team ever in baseball history — but it did come as a disappointment to those hoping for a "Cinderella story" finish.

Cincinnati took the championship the following year as well, sweeping the New York Yankees in four straight games. But in 1977, the Yankees were back on top, thanks to a record-tying performance by one of the game's best players, Reggie Jackson.

Jackson had played in two previous World Series, in 1973 and 1974, as a member of the Oakland Athletics (he would have played in three, but an injury during the playoffs sidelined him prior to the 1972 championship). In 1973, he was named the Series MVP, when his two-run homer in the third inning of the seventh game gave the A's the jump they needed over the New York Mets.

In 1977, Jackson returned to the Series, this time

wearing Yankee pinstripes. Once again, he showed the world what a clutch player he was.

After five games, the Series score stood at New York 3, Los Angeles 2. The Dodgers led game six, 3–2, going into the bottom of the fourth inning. With a runner at first, Jackson came to the plate — and blasted the first pitch thrown for a two-run homer. Then, in the bottom of the fifth inning, he did the same thing again. And then, incredibly, Jackson homered a *third* time, once again sending the first pitch into the stratosphere. Three consecutive at bats, three first pitches, three home runs!

The only other player to hit three homers in a row in the World Series? Babe Ruth. New York won the game 8–4, and pocketed their first championship ring in more than a decade. Jackson pocketed a nickname, "Mr. October," and a place in the history books as the only player ever to hit five home runs in a single Series.

★ CHAPTER EIGHT ★

1980s

1988: "Unbelievable!"

Reggie Jackson's outstanding 1977 World Series performance made him a household name. But sometimes, it's an error that puts a player's name on everyone's lips. In 1986, one man's mistake blackened his reputation for years to come.

According to baseball legend, Babe Ruth had cursed the Boston Red Sox when the team traded him to the Yankees in 1919. That curse, the story went, had prevented the Red Sox from winning a World Series ever since. When the Sox earned a trip back to the October Classic in 1986, everyone hoped they would put the Curse of the Bambino behind them forever.

The Sox were facing the New York Mets, whose 108 wins in the regular season made them the obvious favorites. It came as a huge surprise to the New York team, therefore, when they dropped the first two games before their hometown fans. They roared back the next two, however, to tie the Series at two games apiece, only to see the advantage swing back to the Sox when Boston won game five.

Game six was played in Shea Stadium before a sellout crowd. After nine innings, the score was tied 3–3. Then, at the top of the tenth, leadoff batter Dave Henderson belted a home run to push the Red Sox up by one. Later that inning, slugger Wade Boggs lambasted a double and then came home on a single from Marty Barrett.

With the score 5–3, the Mets came up to bat. When the first two Mets got out, it seemed the Red Sox were about to win their first World Series in sixty-eight years.

But then pitcher Calvin Schiraldi gave up three straight singles. The Mets scored to draw within one. Schiraldi was pulled and reliever Bob Stanley took the mound.

There were two outs, with runners on first and third. Mookie Wilson came up to bat. Stanley worked him to a full count. Then, on the seventh pitch, disaster struck.

The pitch was wild! Kevin Mitchell took off from

third base and hit the dirt in front of home. Safe! The score was all tied up, and Ray Knight, the winning run, was standing on second base.

Stanley faced Wilson again. Wilson fouled off the next two pitches. Then, on the tenth pitch, Wilson connected.

It was a grounder right toward first baseman Bill Buckner. Buckner moved in, ready to scoop up the ball for an easy out. But somehow, unbelievably, the ball rolled *under* Buckner's glove, through his legs, and into the outfield!

The error proved costly, both for Boston and Buckner. As Buckner scrambled to retrieve the ball, Knight took off for home. Safe! The Mets won the game, 6–5. And when New York took the seventh and final game the following day, Boston's hopes of "reversing the Curse" were dashed once again. And Buckner was forever after the most hated player in Red Sox history.

On the flip side of that coin, of course, are the players who, in a single moment, become heroes. In 1988, it was Kirk Gibson of the L.A. Dodgers who earned such a place in baseball history.

Even before Gibson made his mark in the 1988

World Series against the Oakland Athletics, he was already beloved by his fans. One week earlier, Gibson had homered in the twelfth inning of game four of the National League Championship series, breaking the tie to win the game for the Dodgers. The next game, he homered again, this time with two men on base. Those three runs made the difference in the game. The Dodgers went on to win the NLCS, four games to three.

Unfortunately, the pennant race took its toll on Gibson. He suffered injuries to his right knee and a hamstring pull in his left leg. The pain was so great that the star player could barely stand, let alone swing a bat or run the bases.

When the World Series began on October 15, Gibson was in the team training room, nursing his injuries. He cheered as his teammate, Mickey Hatcher, slugged a two-run homer in the first inning — and then groaned as the lead slipped away on a grand-slam home run by Jose Canseco the very next inning.

The Dodgers managed to shave that two-run advantage to one in the sixth, but going into the bottom of the ninth, they were still behind by one. Closer Dennis Eckersley came in to pitch for the

Athletics and promptly retired the first two batters. Oakland was one out away from winning game one.

Then pinch hitter Mike Davis got on base with a walk. With the tying run on first, the Dodgers desperately needed a hit. But they weren't likely to get it from the next scheduled batter, relief pitcher Alejandro Pena. They needed a pinch hitter, someone who could deliver a powerful blast in a clutch. Dave Anderson was available, but manager Tommy Lasorda wasn't sure Anderson was the player for the job.

He wanted Kirk Gibson. And he got him.

The crowd roared and stamped their feet as the burly outfielder, obviously in agony, hobbled to the plate. "You talk about a roll of the dice," said TV announcer Vin Scully. "This is it."

Eckersley worked Gibson to a full count. Then, as Gibson readied himself for the next pitch, something a scout named Mel Didier had told him jumped into his head. Eckersley, Didier had said, had a favorite pitch he liked to throw when he got a lefty in a full count.

"I looked at Eckersley," Gibson later recalled, "and I said, 'Partner, as sure as I'm standing here breathing, you're going to throw me that three-and-two backdoor slider.'"

Gibson called time and stepped out of the box. He took a moment to imagine the slider. Then he stepped back in and waited.

Eckersley went into his windup and threw. Sure enough, it was a slider!

Gibson swung. *Pow!*

"A fly ball to deep right field!" yelled radio announcer Jack Buck. "This is gonna be a home run! Unbelievable! A home run for Gibson! And the Dodgers have won the game, 5–4! I don't believe what I just saw! I don't believe what I just saw!"

Vin Scully was just as excited. "High fly ball hit into right field . . . she is . . . GONE!" the usually soft-spoken announcer bellowed. "The impossible has happened!"

Gibson limped around the bases, grinning from ear to ear and pumping his fists. That blast was the only at bat he had all Series, but it remains to this day one of the most memorable home runs of all baseball history. Perhaps buoyed by Gibson's achievement, the Dodgers went on to win the championship, upsetting the A's four games to one.

☆ CHAPTER NINE ☆

1990s

1991: The Worst-to-First Classic

The 1991 postseason saw two unlikely teams battling for the championship. The Minnesota Twins had had below .500 records for much of the past decade; in 1990, they'd had one of their worst seasons ever, winning only 74 games while dropping 88. The Atlanta Braves were even worse: they'd been in last place for three years running. But in 1991, both teams improved dramatically and, amazingly, clinched spots in the World Series.

The Braves hadn't been to the championship since 1957, when they'd been Milwaukee's home team; the closest they'd come was a division win in 1982. When they entered Minnesota's Metrodome for the start of the 88th World Series, they were eager to erase decades of subpar seasons.

Of course, the Twins were equally eager for victory. And that first game, they got what they wanted. The final score of the game was Twins 5, Braves 2.

The two clubs met in the Metrodome again the next day. The Braves' starting pitcher was Tom Glavine, who, after a shaky start his rookie season in 1988, went on to win twenty games in 1991. For the Twins, it was Kevin Tapani on the mound. Tapani had had six consecutive losses early in the 1991 season before pulling out of his slump to win eleven of his last thirteen games.

Tapani retired Atlanta's first three batters in order. Glavine, on the other hand, was hit by the first batter he faced, Dan Gladden. Gladden's shallow fly ball should have been an easy out, but instead, he made it all the way to second when right fielder David Justice and second baseman Mark Lemke collided going for the catch. Then Glavine walked Chuck Knoblauch, bringing up heavy hitter Kirby Puckett with two men on.

With 15 home runs in 1991, Puckett was a very real threat. This time up, he swung so hard that he broke the bat! As the bat's head and the ball both flew toward third base, Puckett flew toward first,

Knoblauch toward second, and Gladden toward third.

But third baseman Terry Pendleton was ready. He nabbed the ball and stepped on third to get Gladden out. Then he fired the ball to first. Double play! Puckett returned to the dugout. Knoblauch, meanwhile, stood at second.

He didn't stay there for long. The Twins' designated hitter, Chili Davis, slammed a home run to left center field. Both Chuck and Chili crossed home plate.

Atlanta got on the board the next inning with a single run. The score was still 2–1 when the Braves came up again in the top of the third. Leadoff batter Rafael Belliard grounded out. Lonnie Smith made it to first on an error by third baseman Scott Leius. He stayed there when Terry Pendleton flied out.

With two outs and Smith at first, Ron Gant singled to left. The hit was good enough for Smith to make it to third. Gant, meanwhile, rounded first base and then, realizing that Tapani was about to pick him off with a throw to first, jumped back to the bag. At that same moment, first baseman Kent Hrbek reached forward for the ball.

At more than 250 pounds, Hrbek was a big man with aspirations of becoming a professional wrestler someday. Gant weighed in at just above 170. When the two met by the bag, Hrbek used his brawn to lift Gant by the leg as he tagged him!

With that strange out, the Braves' chances of tying the game that inning were over. But in the fifth inning, they scored their second run to make it 2–2. That's how things stayed until the bottom of the eighth, when the Twins' rookie third baseman, Scott Leius, sent Glavine's first pitch soaring over the left-field wall. The home run gave the Twins the lead, a lead they kept until the game's end.

The championship moved to Atlanta for game three. It was the first-ever World Series game played in Fulton County Stadium, and the Braves wanted to give their fans something to cheer about. But at first, the fans did nothing but groan.

Atlanta's Steve Avery was on the mound. The 21-year-old had an 18–8 regular season record and a ninety-eight-mile-per-hour fastball. At the start of the game, he also had a severe case of the jitters. He gave up a triple to leadoff batter Dan Gladden, then saw Gladden race home on a sacrifice fly. Two batters and it was already 1–0!

Fortunately for the Braves, Avery got the next two out. The following inning, he sent the batters down in order. He did the same thing the next three innings. In all, Avery dispatched fifteen in a row, five of which were strikeouts! The Braves, meanwhile, had chalked up four runs to make it a 4–1 ball game.

But by the eighth inning, the Twins tied it up, 4–4. The score stayed that way through the bottom of the ninth. In the tenth inning, both teams threatened to push over the winning run, but failed. The score remained 4–4 through the eleventh, forcing a twelfth.

Tension mounted as the Twins loaded the bases with two outs. A good hit now could win the game. But the chance of getting that hit seemed slim. They were out of pinch hitters and were faced with batting either relief pitcher Mark Guthrie, who had never batted in a game, or reliever Rick Aguilera, who had. They chose Aguilera.

Aguilera connected for a line drive to left. The runners took off at full speed — and then slowed to a halt. Ron Gant had caught the ball for the third out.

The game had been going on for more than four hours. It finally ended in the bottom of the twelfth. With bases loaded, two outs, Mark Lemke belted a single over short that was just strong enough to score David Justice. The Braves won the game, turning what might have been a three-game deficit into a two-to-one Series.

Then, amazingly, two nights later, the Series stood at three to two! Game four had been another triumph for Mark Lemke, whose ninth-inning triple scored the tying run and put him in position to make the winning run — which he made after tagging up and beating a throw home.

By comparison, game five wasn't quite as exciting, unless you considered watching the home team completely destroy the visitors 14–5 exciting. Of course, after the close shaves of the last two games, that margin was just fine with the Braves and their fans!

The two teams returned to Minnesota for game six, another extra-innings, edge-of-the-seat finish.

It was the bottom of the eleventh. The score had been tied at 3–3 for a grueling four-and-a-half innings. Both teams were exhausted, but with the championship on the line, neither was about to give up.

Relief pitcher Charlie Leibrandt took the mound for the Braves. Kirby Puckett was in the batter's box. It was the third time the two players had faced one another in the Series. In the two previous meetings, Puckett had struck out on Leibrandt's changeup. He was determined not to be fooled by the same pitch again. When the same pitch came, Puckett blasted it far into center field. Home run!

The hit marked the fourth one-run victory of the Series. Fans who liked down-to-the-wire excitement had had more than their fill with this championship — and that was before game seven was even played.

Game seven, according to baseball watchers everywhere, was one of the most memorable ever played. It was a pitcher's duel, pitting twenty-four-year-old John Smoltz of the Atlanta Braves against a man he had admired growing up, veteran hurler Jack Morris. There was a twelve-year difference in their ages, but statistically, they were near equals.

Just how equal was evident right from the start. Morris retired the first six batters he faced. Smoltz sent four back to the dugout before giving up two singles. He defused the scoring threat, however, by covering first on the next play to end the inning.

Inning after inning it went on. Batters who got hits died on base. After seven innings, the scoreboard showed nothing but goose eggs. The anticipation was almost palpable: Who, fans and players wondered, would finally break through?

The answer almost came at the top of the eighth. Lonnie Smith singled to right, bringing up Terry Pendleton. With a mighty swing, Pendleton blasted the ball deep into left center field.

Braves fans jumped up, eyes glued to the ball's path. If it went over the wall, it was a ground-rule double that would prevent Smith from rounding third and heading home. If it rebounded off the wall, it could still be a double, but maybe good enough to get Smith across the plate.

Blam! The ball hit and bounced back to the field. The crowd cheered and shifted their gaze to Smith, not wanting to miss the moment he hit the dirt in front of home plate.

But to their horror, Smith wasn't running home. Even though the ball was still far in the outfield, he was stopping at third!

What had happened? The answer was simple if astonishing.

When Pendleton had hit the ball, Smith took off from first without knowing where the ball was headed. As Smith passed second, he saw infielder Chuck Knoblauch field the ball and throw it to Greg Gagne, who was covering second. Smith stopped at third, certain he was lucky to have made it there safely.

But of course, Gagne didn't have the ball. Smith had been tricked by a classic decoy play!

Morris finished off the Braves, sending them back into the field without a run.

Unfortunately for the Twins, the Braves did the same to them. At the top of the ninth, the score was still 0–0.

And then, incredibly, at the end of the bottom of the ninth, it was *still* 0–0.

Morris took the mound for the tenth inning, making him the only other pitcher besides Christy Mathewson to pitch for more than nine in a World Series. He had faced thirty-five batters so far. He faced three more now, retiring the side in order. Now it was up to his teammates to bring it on home.

In the Braves dugout, Smoltz watched the action unfold. He had lasted nearly eight innings. Now Alejandro Pena was pitching. Pena had held the

Twins scoreless so far, and was determined to the same this inning.

But the first batter he faced, Dan Gladden, sent the ball soaring into left field. Gladden stretched the hit into a double. Then Chuck Knoblauch bunted down the third baseline. Knoblauch was out, but Gladden was safe at third.

Pena walked sluggers Kirby Puckett and Kent Hrbek. The bases were loaded, with still only one out.

As the clock ticked onto midnight, Eugene Larkin came up to bat. Larkin knew what he had to do: hit a ball high enough so that Gladden could tag up and beat the throw home.

The Braves knew what he needed to do, too. But knowing it and preventing it are two different things.

Pena threw and Larkin connected, not for a simple fly ball but for a long blast into left field. Outfielder Brian Hunter started for it and then stopped, knowing full well that that hit had just scored the Series-winning run.

As the Twins swarmed out of the dugout, the Braves slowly walked off the field. Yet even in defeat, the Atlanta team took comfort in knowing that they'd been part of the most memorable Series ever played. Mark Lemke summed it up best when he said, "Man, that was fun. Let's do it again next year!"

Lemke and the Braves would, indeed, "do it again next year," winning the pennant but losing the World Series to the Blue Jays. In 1993, the Blue Jays won again, besting the Philadelphia Phillies four games to two.

Then, in 1994, a long-simmering conflict between players and owners boiled over. The season was cut short when the players went on strike on August 12 to protest the team owners' call for a cap on salaries. On September 9, baseball commissioner Bud Selig was forced to cancel the remainder of the season, including the postseason championship. For the first time ever, there would be no World Series.

Baseball fans were appalled, especially since greed seemed at the heart of the strike. Baseball's reputation took a severe beating in the following months; in fact, it would take a few years before it rebuilt its fan base to what it had once been.

But rebuild it did, thanks in large part to classic baseball drama. The New York Yankees regained their long-lost throne in 1996, lost it in 1997, and then claimed it again in 1998 and 1999. In 1997, the tenth-inning, seventh-game World Series triumph of the upstart Florida Marlins over the Cleveland Indians had fans cheering in the streets. And in the final months of the 1998 regular season, the world watched as Mark McGwire and Sammy Sosa raced to beat Roger Maris's home-run record.

By the start of the new millennium, most baseball fans had put the players' strike behind them. They were ready to sit back and enjoy the national pastime once again.

★ CHAPTER TEN ★

2000s

2004 and 2005: What Curses?

The first World Series of the millennium ended the way the last one of the old millennium had — with a victory by the New York Yankees. But in 2001, the mighty Yanks were put down by the Arizona Diamondbacks, a team that had been in existence for only three years! New York was out of the running the following year but returned to the fall classic in 2003 — only to lose once again, this time to the Florida Marlins.

Then came 2004 and with it one of the most unexpected and thrilling postseason upsets baseball had ever seen.

The Boston Red Sox had been a "close but no cigar" club since the mid-1980s. In 2004, they came out on top in the American League East with a record of 98 wins, 64 losses. In the postseason, they quickly dispatched the Anaheim Angels for the Division title. Next up, however, were the Yankees, their longtime rivals and, with a record of 101–61, the better of the two teams.

The first two games of the ALCS were played in New York. The Sox lost both. The series moved to Fenway Park for game three — which the Sox also lost by a demoralizing 19–8!

The Yankees needed only one victory to move on to the World Series. They didn't get it in game four, however. Instead, Boston squeaked out a twelfth-inning win thanks to a two-run homer by power hitter David Ortiz.

Ortiz was the man of the hour again in game five — a very late hour at that, for he blasted an RBI single in the *fourteenth* inning to give the Sox a 5–4 win. The next night, back in Yankee Stadium, a home run by Mark Bellhorn in the fourth inning handed the Sox their third straight victory.

The next game, Boston made history by doing what no team had ever done. They fought back from a 3–0 deficit to win four straight games. It was an unbelievable feat, made all the more thrilling by the game-saving home runs and the incredible stamina of injured pitcher Curt Schilling, whose right ankle was noticeably bloody throughout much of his game-six win.

The "Boston Faithful," as Red Sox fans called themselves, were overjoyed. Banners reading RE-VERSE THE CURSE! flew from bridges, out of windows, and scrawled across newspapers. All of Boston hoped this would be the year the legendary Curse of the Bambino would finally be put to bed.

After the suspenseful come-from-behind success story of the ALCS, the 2004 World Series between the St. Louis Cardinals and the Boston Red Sox was somewhat tame.

Somewhat, but not completely.

The first game was a shoot-out started by David Ortiz, who belted a three-run homer in his first at bat. Boston posted another run later in the inning to go ahead by four. Then, in the bottom of the third, a series of well-hit singles added three more runs to Boston's side.

The Cardinals, meanwhile, had crossed home plate only twice. But they came roaring back, and by the bottom of the sixth inning, the score was tied, 7–7.

Boston answered their next time up with two of

their own, however, to go ahead 9–7. But then St. Louis pushed across two more in the top of the eighth, tying things up once again!

Mark Bellhorn turned the tide in Boston's favor. With Jason Varitek on first following a fielding error, he rang the right-field pole on a pitch by Julián Tavárez. Home run!

The Sox were up, 11–9, and when Red Sox closer Keith Foulke retired St. Louis in the top of the ninth, Boston had their first World Series game tucked neatly in their back pockets.

Three nights and two victories later, the Red Sox were one win away from sweeping the Cardinals out of the Series and capturing their first championship ring in eighty-six years.

Game four was played in Busch Stadium before a sellout crowd. The night air had a hint of magic in it, for a full lunar eclipse was predicted to occur during the game. As the moon slowly began to disappear behind the shadow of the Earth, Red Sox leadoff batter Johnny Damon came to the plate. He took a called strike and two balls and then, on the fourth pitch, did what only sixteen other leadoff batters have done in the World Series: he hit a home run! One at bat and Boston was already on the board!

The Sox sweetened the lead by two in the top of the third, thanks to a two-run double by Trot Nixon. Meanwhile, pitcher Derek Lowe was busy blanking the Cardinals inning after inning. When he finally came out of the game after the seventh inning, he had given up only three hits!

All Boston needed was to hold St. Louis for two more innings. They did just that — and when Edgar Renteria grounded out to end the bottom of the ninth, the Red Sox had finally put the eighty-six-year-old Curse behind them!

Players and fans went wild. Corks popped in the locker room, and champagne sprayed everyone around. Johnny Damon spoke for the whole team by saying, "We're going to enjoy it a bit . . . and do what champions do — celebrate!"

The following year, it was the other Sox team that was celebrating, however. Like their East Coast cousins, the Chicago White Sox hadn't won a World Series in more than eight decades. They, too, had a curse to overcome: the Black Sox Scandal of 1919.

In 2005, they did just what the Red Sox had done — they put that curse to bed by sweeping their opponents, the Houston Astros, in four straight games to win their first World Series in eighty-eight years.

The final nail in the Astros' coffin came in classic style. It was the eighth inning of game four. The White Sox were up at bat. The score was tied 0–0. There were two outs. Willie Harris stood at third, ready to run for home.

Jermaine Dye came up to the plate. He swung at pitcher Brad Lidge's first offering. Strike one. The second pitch was in the dirt for ball one, but the third pitch was on the money. Dye swung.

Pow! Ground ball to center field! Dye rushed for first, and Harris sprinted for home — and made it!

That single run was the only one of the game. With it, the White Sox erased their past mistakes and, like the 102 World Series winners before them, were welcomed home as heroes.

The World Series is now more than a century old. Professional baseball is even older. The sport has had its share of low points, from the 1919 Black Sox scandal to the present-day issue of illegal steroid use in the major leagues.

Yet despite these setbacks, people the world over continue to look forward to the start of baseball season with eager anticipation. Fans talk about the players as if they were old friends — or bitter enemies. They compare statistics on their favorite players, past and current. And they relive their favorite plays, including classic World Series moments.

Babe Ruth's legendary Called Shot. Jackie Robinson stealing home. Carlton Fisk waving the ball fair. Kirk Gibson hobbling around the bases. Mention errors like Fred Snodgrass's dropped shot and Billy Buckner's failure to field an easy grounder to a true baseball fan, and you're certain to get a heated response.

There's just something about the sport — the crack of the bat that signals a home run, the suspense of the no-hitter, the split second before the umpire calls the runner safe or out — that keeps people coming back for more. As Hall-of-Famer Rogers Hornsby once said, "People ask me what I do in winter when there's no baseball. I'll tell you what I do. I stare out the window and wait for spring."

World Series Results

1900s

1903   Boston Red Sox 5, Pittsburgh 3

1904   Not Held

1905   New York Giants 4, Philadelphia A's 1

1906   Chicago White Sox 4, Chicago Cubs 2

1907   Chicago Cubs 4, Detroit 0 (one tie)

1908   Chicago Cubs 4, Detroit 1

1909   Pittsburgh 4, Detroit 3

1910   Philadelphia A's 4, Chicago Cubs 1

1911   Philadelphia A's 4, New York Giants 2

1912   Boston Red Sox 4, New York Giants 3 (one tie)

1913   Philadelphia A's 4, New York Giants 1

1914   Boston Braves 4, Philadelphia A's 0

1915   Boston Red Sox 4, Philadelphia Phillies 1

1916   Boston Red Sox 4, Brooklyn 1

1917   Chicago White Sox 4, New York Giants 2

1918   Boston Red Sox 4, Chicago Cubs 2

1919   Cincinnati 5, Chicago White Sox 3

1920s

1920   Cleveland 5, Brooklyn 2

1921   New York Giants 5, New York Yankees 3

1922   New York Giants 4, New York Yankees 0 (one tie)

1923	New York Yankees 4, New York Giants 2
1924	Washington 4, New York Giants 3
1925	Pittsburgh 4, Washington 3
1926	St. Louis Cardinals 4, New York Yankees 3
1927	New York Yankees 4, Pittsburgh 0
1928	New York Yankees 4, St. Louis Cardinals 0
1929	Philadelphia A's 4, Chicago Cubs 1

1930s

1930	Philadelphia A's 4, St. Louis Cardinals 2
1931	St. Louis Cardinals 4, Philadelphia A's 3
1932	New York Yankees 4, Chicago Cubs 0
1933	New York Giants 4, Washington 1
1934	St. Louis Cardinals 4, Detroit 3
1935	Detroit 4, Chicago Cubs 2
1936	New York Yankees 4, New York Giants 2
1937	New York Yankees 4, New York Giants 1
1938	New York Yankees 4, Chicago Cubs 0
1939	New York Yankees 4, Cincinnati 0

1940s

1940	Cincinnati 4, Detroit 3
1941	New York Yankees 4, Brooklyn 1
1942	St. Louis Cardinals 4, New York Yankees 1
1943	New York Yankees 4, St. Louis Cardinals 1
1944	St. Louis Cardinals 4, St. Louis Browns 2

1945	Detroit 4, Chicago Cubs 3
1946	St. Louis Cardinals 4, Boston Red Sox 3
1947	New York Yankees 4, Brooklyn 3
1948	Cleveland 4, Boston Braves 2
1949	New York Yankees 4, Brooklyn 1

1950s

1950	New York Yankees 4, Philadelphia 0
1951	New York Yankees 4, New York Giants 2
1952	New York Yankees 4, Brooklyn 3
1953	New York Yankees 4, Brooklyn 2
1954	New York Giants 4, Cleveland 0
1955	Brooklyn 4, New York Yankees 3
1956	New York Yankees 4, Brooklyn 3
1957	Milwaukee Braves 4, New York Yankees 3
1958	New York Yankees 4, Milwaukee Braves 3
1959	Los Angeles 4, Chicago White Sox 2

1960s

1960	Pittsburgh 4, New York Yankees 3
1961	New York Yankees 4, Cincinnati 1
1962	New York Yankees 4, San Francisco 3
1963	Los Angeles 4, New York Yankees 0
1964	St. Louis 4, New York Yankees 3
1965	Los Angeles 4, Minnesota 3
1966	Baltimore 4, Los Angeles 0

1967	St. Louis 4, Boston 3
1968	Detroit 4, St. Louis 3
1969	New York Mets 4, Baltimore 1

1970s

1970	Baltimore 4, Cincinnati 1
1971	Pittsburgh 4, Baltimore 3
1972	Oakland 4, Cincinnati 3
1973	Oakland 4, New York Mets 3
1974	Oakland 4, Los Angeles 1
1975	Cincinnati 4, Boston 3
1976	Cincinnati 4, New York Yankees 0
1977	New York Yankees 4, Los Angeles 2
1978	New York Yankees 4, Los Angeles 2
1979	Pittsburgh 4, Baltimore 3

1980s

1980	Philadelphia 4, Kansas City 2
1981	Los Angeles 4, New York Yankees 2
1982	St. Louis 4, Milwaukee 3
1983	Baltimore 4, Philadelphia 1
1984	Detroit 4, San Diego 1
1985	Kansas City 4, St. Louis 3
1986	New York Mets 4, Boston 3
1987	Minnesota 4, St. Louis 3
1988	Los Angeles 4, Oakland 1

1989	Oakland 4, San Francisco 0
1990s	
1990	Cincinnati 4, Oakland 0
1991	Minnesota 4, Atlanta 3
1992	Toronto 4, Atlanta 2
1993	Toronto 4, Philadelphia 2
1994	Not Held
1995	Atlanta 4, Cleveland 2
1996	New York Yankees 4, Atlanta 2
1997	Florida 4, Cleveland 3
1998	New York Yankees 4, San Diego 0
1999	New York Yankees 4, Atlanta 0
2000s	
2000	New York Yankees 4, New York Mets 1
2001	Arizona 4, New York Yankees 3
2002	Anaheim 4, San Francisco 3
2003	Florida 4, New York Yankees 2
2004	Boston 4, St. Louis 0
2005	Chicago White Sox 4, Houston 0

Matt Christopher®

Sports Bio Bookshelf

Muhammad Ali

Lance Armstrong

Kobe Bryant

Jennifer Capriati

Jeff Gordon

Ken Griffey Jr.

Mia Hamm

Tony Hawk

Ichiro

Derek Jeter

Randy Johnson

Michael Jordan

Mario Lemieux

Tara Lipinski

Mark McGwire

Yao Ming

Shaquille O'Neal

Jackie Robinson

Alex Rodriguez

Babe Ruth

Curt Schilling

Sammy Sosa

Venus and Serena Williams

Tiger Woods

The #1
Sports Series
for Kids

Read them all!

- Baseball Pals
- Baseball Turnaround
- The Basket Counts
- Body Check
- Catch That Pass!
- Catcher with a Glass Arm
- Catching Waves
- Center Court Sting
- Centerfield Ballhawk
- Challenge at Second Base
- The Comeback Challenge
- Comeback of the Home Run Kid
- Cool as Ice
- The Diamond Champs
- Dirt Bike Racer
- Dirt Bike Runaway

- Dive Right In
- Double Play at Short
- Face-Off
- Fairway Phenom
- Football Fugitive
- Football Nightmare
- The Fox Steals Home
- Goalkeeper in Charge
- The Great Quarterback Switch
- Halfback Attack*
- The Hockey Machine
- Ice Magic
- Inline Skater
- Johnny Long Legs
- The Kid Who Only Hit Homers
- Lacrosse Face-Off

*Previously published as Crackerjack Halfback

Line Drive to Short**

Long-Arm Quarterback

Long Shot for Paul

Look Who's Playing First Base

Miracle at the Plate

Mountain Bike Mania

No Arm in Left Field

Nothin' But Net

Penalty Shot

Prime-Time Pitcher

Red-Hot Hightops

The Reluctant Pitcher

Return of the Home Run Kid

Roller Hockey Radicals

Run For It

Shoot for the Hoop

Shortstop from Tokyo

Skateboard Renegade

Skateboard Tough

Slam Dunk

Snowboard Champ

Snowboard Maverick

Snowboard Showdown

Soccer Duel

Soccer Halfback

Soccer Scoop

Stealing Home

The Submarine Pitch

The Team That Couldn't Lose

Tennis Ace

Tight End

Top Wing

Touchdown for Tommy

Tough to Tackle

Wheel Wizards

Windmill Windup

Wingman on Ice

The Year Mom Won the Pennant

All available in paperback from Little, Brown and Company

**Previously published as Pressure Play